JORGE LOYZAGA

JORGE LOYZAGA

Classical and Harmonic Proportions
Architecture of a Gracious Lifestyle

Photography by Mauricio de la Garza Clariond
Text by Philip Alvaré

RIZZOLI NEW YORK

New York · Paris · London · Milan

Contents

Jorge Loyzaga
The Transformative Power of Classical Design

When Jorge Loyzaga speaks of the relationship he develops with each client, he refers to *protocolos de vida*—the protocols of life, a term often reserved for procedures and rules for diplomatic occasions and accepted codes of behavior. Every house he designs represents a relationship with his clients. He reflects, "Every house is in some way a form of psychoanalysis, a psychology in stone, a petrified analysis. When the client turns and sees the house, they begin to understand who they will become."

The French philosopher, Gaston Bachelard, evoked a similar theme in his book, *The Poetics of Space*, and the concept of topoanalysis, the study of human identity and how that relates to our lives through analysis of personal and emotional responses to our domestic environment.

"The context of houses designed with classical proportions and harmonics as well as the use of fine materials," explains Loyzaga, "uplifts the quality of life and often the clients' social standing in the community. It has the power of transformation to change your environment and life. It changes people." There is something of the magician about Jorge Loyzaga.

Many of Jorge Loyzaga's clients are second and third generation, children and grandchildren of people he worked with over the past fifty years. The son of one former client speaks of the house designed for his parents as ". . . a temple and haven. I would even say Jorge's spaces are uplifting, monastic, and invite inhabitants toward contemplation, meditation, and a reverence for nature." Other clients commission Jorge Loyzaga to create one of his extraordinary and ultimately habitable domestic environments where notable collections of art, fine antiques, and decorative objects converge exquisitely within the Loyzaga environment.

"Houses designed and constructed using classical proportion have the power of human scale and harmonic balance derived from nature," he offers. "A modern house from the 1950s can be alienating. But the elegance of classical proportion, scale, and harmonics enhances the social environment. It's an environment to enrich the story of the family that transmits a cultural understanding. It teaches, imparts knowledge and values, and incites transformation." The materials used are natural and elemental with masterfully handcrafted wood, stone, and iron embellishments as opposed to prefabricated synthetics.

The arrangement of elements in a kitchen, for example, with a fine pantry of ample proportion, custom cabinetry, traditional assortment of china, stemware, and cutlery transforms the way we live. The design imparts protocols of life that furthers appreciation, and enjoyment. Similarly, the presentation of art, furniture, and decorative objects arranged in a harmonious way imparts a gracious way of life conducive to hosting and entertaining.

More than a few Loyzaga Studio clients are impresarios—CEOs with diplomatic responsibilities who see an ambassadorial aspect to their homes as a vehicle to present Mexican culture and tradition through the assemblage of various elements within their residences. In this manner, Jorge Loyzaga has revived not only the lost art of fine craftsmanship, but the lost art of gracious living as well.

Loyzaga also speaks of comportment, a term not currently in common use that suggests behavior and bearing calling to mind *Emily Post's Etiquette*, an instruction manual for polite society in the United States. A proper guestroom must be equipped with certain essential items—a writing table, letterhead, a carafe of water on the nightstand, a good book, sufficient wardrobe space, and an ample chest of drawers. The manual contains diagrams illustrating correct table settings for luncheons and dinner parties with exacting placement for each utensil—fish knives and oyster forks—down to the runcible spoon. It provides invaluable information for those interested in bettering themselves.

Edith Wharton's *The Decoration of Houses* also springs to mind. Her splendid estate, The Mount, in the Berkshire Mountains of Western Massachusetts, with its Palladian proportions and Italianate gardens, epitomizes the aspirations of a new, well-heeled, American breed at the turn of the nineteenth and twentieth centuries determined to emulate haute European society. And while notions of comportment, manners, protocols, and politesse seem to have fallen out of fashion, Jorge Loyzaga continues to design houses with those things in mind. He contends, "The houses, arrangement of rooms, furnishings, and decorations are instruments. The design and circulation is instructive without being overly pedantic." He advises his clients and determines how they want to live, what they want to collect, what they want to represent and project. He is the ultimate lifestyle coach.

Jorge Loyzaga's illustrious career spans over half a century and includes residential architecture, restoration of historic monuments, and interior design and conservation projects on four continents. More recently, Loyzaga Studio created a line of furniture and decorative objects under the eponymous brand.

While the portfolio of sumptuous houses and interiors presented in this monograph exhibit a preponderance of styles—an impressive array that encompasses Mexican colonial, French neoclassical, Italian Renaissance, and English Tudor designs, to mention a few, each magnificent residence, regardless of style, radiates a core principle of classical proportion and harmonics. Those principles resonate throughout decorative details as well, with masterfully crafted materials, inlaid marble, sculpted stone, fine carpentry, decorative plasterwork, murals, and bronze adornments. They are equally evident in furnishings and decorations, which give each property a cohesive and harmonious character.

Loyzaga's expertise was forged through years of study and practice. He is a renowned scholar on decoration, conservation, and restoration—a veritable lexicon of period and style. His passion for architecture and design was ignited as a young man on excursions throughout Mexico to explore different villages and learn about different styles. No doubt this had a seminal impact upon the budding architect.

In Mexico, the well of history is deep. Time is measured not just in centuries, but millennia—a vast horizon of more than three thousand years of continuous indigenous cultures, including Maya and Aztec civilizations, supplanted by five hundred years of Spanish and European influence. Certainly, that environment informed Loyzaga's penchant for fluidity of period and style reflected in the array of houses he designed including a Balinese pavilion, an English Jacobean manse, an Italian Renaissance villa, and a French Napoleon III manoir.

Furthermore, there are staggering juxtapositions in Mexico. Spanish baroque palaces and cathedrals are dwarfed alongside Aztec pyramids. The Zócalo, or main square of Mexico City, once the center of the Spanish Viceregal Court in New Spain, is literally built on top of Tenochtilán, the ancient capital of the Aztec empire. The highly mannered, churrigueresque style of late Spanish baroque flourished elaborately in Mexico, uniting carved symbols echoing Maya-Azteca cosmogonies with Spanish Catholic iconography created by indigenous artisans.

Moreover, the Spanish were no strangers to cultural fusion, and Spanish architecture demands consideration of Hispano-Arabic culture and style. Arab Spain, Al-Andalus, endured for eight hundred years and much of that aesthetic tradition was transmitted to Mexico through Mudéjar style. All of these influences resonate throughout the houses created by Jorge Loyzaga.

And to those unfamiliar with Mexican history, it may come as a surprise to learn that Maximilian von Habsburg, the Austrian Archduke, reigned as Emperor of the Second Mexican Empire from April 10, 1864, until his execution on June 19, 1867. He and his consort, Carlota, were briefly ensconced in Chapultepec Castle, a neoclassical palace originally constructed as the summer residence for Spanish viceroyalty in Mexico City. Maximilian and Carlota remodeled the castle to suit their Austrian sensibilities.

And unsurprisingly, due to his profound knowledge of decorative and architectural history, Jorge Loyzaga directed the restoration for the interior design and gardens of the neoclassical castle, true to the royal couple's taste. Neoclassicism continued to flourish in Mexico, especially under Porfirio Díaz's presidency from 1876 to 1911, a period referred to as Porfiriato when all things French became the dernier cri. And it is interesting to note Díaz died in Paris and is buried in Cimetière de Montparnasse.

French neoclassical and beaux arts influences are especially pronounced in fashionable Colona Roma in Mexico City, where elegant residences along a grid of avenues recalling Haussmann's Paris confirm the Francophile era. Given the kaleidoscopic aesthetic context in Mexico, especially French neoclassical influence, is it any wonder the young man with a burning passion for architecture would choose a classical approach to design and become a wizard of styles? And when an aunt told him about the school of classical architecture at the University of Santiago de Compostela in Spain, he went there to study architecture and historic restoration.

He recounts the rigorous program with a sparkle in his eye: "We learned about restoration through intensive study of all aspects and components of classical architecture. You must know how to construct a Romanesque arch before knowing how to restore one. It was a nineteenth-century approach and we learned to construct anything from Mudéjar ceilings to English Tudor roofs, everything from moldings to Gothic proportions."

They calculated the proportions of stone through the ancient tradition of geometric sketches without the aid of computers or advanced mathematics. Through trial and error, they learned how to design every arch and element in a staggering array of periods and styles, including Greco-Roman classical architecture, Gothic, Renaissance, baroque, and eighteenth- and nineteenth-century styles. It made a deep, lasting impression that informed—still informs—the classical approach to architecture and design that is the hallmark of Loyzaga Studio currently under the collaborative direction of the architect's twin daughters, Sophia and Fernanda.

In subsequent years, the scholarly architect taught at the distinguished University of Ibero Americana and UNAM in Mexico City. He developed a treatise comparing congruencies among Mayan and Aztec architecture and classical proportions. This furthered his conviction that the principles of classical architecture were universal and transcendent and spanned all cultures, periods, and styles regardless of geographic or cultural context. Further studies of Asian architecture revealed similar congruencies resonating throughout Hindu, Chinese, and Japanese architecture as well.

Though classical architecture is often dismissed as a construct of Western Civilization, it is based upon nature. The Parthenon is usually cited as the prototype and its proportions may be expressed mathematically through the Fibonacci series and geometric proportion of the golden section as the ratio of 1:1.61. The same mathematical proportions can be applied to the structure of a nautilus shell, or the whorled pattern of seeds in a sunflower.

Classical design was codified further by Vitruvius, in his multivolume work *De Architectura* (30–20 BCE), about perfect proportion in architecture based on the human body, which led to Leonardo da Vinci's drawing of the *Vitruvian Man*. As well, Jorge Loyzaga asserts, "You have to use imagination to develop something in architecture, but the root is always the same—the basis, the forms are derived from nature."

The nascent designer's education also included music theory to further understand the concept of harmonics and its relationship to architectural proportions and the application of musical theory for scale, harmony, and the enunciation of different tones and colors. And while we don't have to know how every note and phrase was constructed to appreciate and enjoy the extraordinary houses presented in the following pages, we benefit from the feelings evoked through this type of harmony. It informs the interdependency of all elements, from window casings to rooftops, to arabesque patterns, or to the geometry of a parterre garden. Cohesiveness is achieved through harmonic proportions that transmit feelings of peace and well-being.

The classical approach is also evident through the pattern of compression and release, variations of light, the rhythm of a colonnade, and the sequence of rooms and unfolding spaces, which as in musical composition, transmit and evoke an emotional response.

After twelve years of extensive study in Spain that also included philosophy and psychology to more fully understand human emotions and how to project those things through architecture, the astute Loyzaga worked extensively throughout Europe on a variety of historic restoration projects of World Heritage Sites in conjunction with UNESCO. Then, eventually, he returned home to Mexico.

His extensive experience with architectural restoration served him well and led to collaboration with architects from the Instituto Classico and involvement with the Center for Inter-American Relations at 680 Park Avenue in New York. The handsome edifice is one along a block of notable mansions designed by architects McKim, Mead & White. The Marquesa de Cuevas, formerly Margaret Rockefeller Strong, purchased it to rescue it from demolition circa 1965, then donated it to the Center for Inter-American Relations under the Landmarks Law. It is now listed on the National Register of Historic Properties.

It was a fortuitous confluence of events for Jorge Loyzaga, in that he realized the American Renaissance Style championed by McKim, Mead & White reflected the same classical training and applied design skills in which he had been rigorously schooled. Moreover, he could apply his knowledge to produce new residential architecture in the classical tradition.

Soon after, the perspicacious Loyzaga received his first major residential commission from a lady who wanted a house built in Mexico City in the late eighteenth-century French neoclassical style. Apparently, it made quite a splash, and she soon found herself entertaining a smart set, including the French Ambassador to Mexico.

The ambassador was duly impressed by the elegant verisimilitude of her mansion and the cultivated taste it projected true to the late eighteenth-century French tradition. Eventually, he bought it on behalf of the French government, including all the furnishings and decorations, and it became the French Embassy in Mexico. And the lady turned a handsome profit. The same woman commissioned the young architect again, this time to design an Italian villa in Acapulco, Mexico, which was sufficiently elegant to enable her to entertain Italian aristocrats and heads of state. People took note, and Jorge Loyzaga became fully aware of the correlation between domestic environment and social standing.

From that point on, his career ascended. Soon, friends of the woman who had commissioned him to design her houses in the French and Italian tastes wanted the emerging favorite to design their houses as well. It was an opportune moment for the fledging, classically trained architect because some people had already begun to weary of mid-century modernism.

Another notable commission arrived from the scion of a grand old Mexican family. The gentleman wanted to renovate the family's seigneurial home near the ancient ruins of Teotihuacán. The formidable place had been designed in the traditionally austere manner of eighteenth-century Mexican colonial haciendas. The now-esteemed architect repurposed the grand old hacienda to a level of elegance suitable for entertaining royalty. At that point, Jorge Loyzaga fully grasped the idea that designing an environment to create an ambiance in which a gracious way of life can flourish serves as an instrument that allows people to engage at the highest level of cultivated society.

Today, the Loyzaga Studio and showroom is situated in San Miguel Chapultepec, a neighborhood in Mexico City where there are alleys within alleys. The nearly nondescript warehouse-like façade belies the space within that possesses a cloistered calm. A passageway leads to a courtyard where a three-story neoclassical edifice rises like a dream. A series of rooms arranged off the central axis, a reception area, sample room, library, and Jorge Loyzaga's office, seem to embody the erudite contours of the architect's mind. All told, there are over thirty thousand volumes throughout the studio.

In his office, Jorge Loyzaga recounts how in the nineteenth century, the Academy of San Carlos in Mexico City taught Classical Arts at a satellite campus at the Sorbonne in Paris, where students learned the French neoclassical approach to architecture. Those architects developed Colonia Roma with its elegant avenues anchored by handsome buildings in the French neoclassical style.

But, the French-trained architects could not find artisans with skills necessary to create the elaborate wrought iron, masterfully carved stone, fine carpentry, and specialized finishes required to realize their designs in Mexico. However it wasn't for lack of talent as evidenced by Classic period Mayan stonework rivaling the most elaborate European rococo ornamentation. Nevertheless, master artisans arrived from France to teach time-honored techniques. They developed workshops and studios in the Renaissance tradition of trade guilds.

Similarly, as Jorge Loyzaga's reputation flourished, he found himself increasingly in demand with a shortage of skilled artisans. Well aware of the extraordinary talent pool and ancient crafts tradition in Mexico, he recalled the San Carlos model and developed his own workshops for individual trades to realize his designs and create the outstanding decorative elements and details for which he became renowned. In addition, a providential venture with a colleague in the Philippines, part of the Spanish Empire during the viceregal period, presented an opportunity to train additional Mexican artisans to realize the exacting level of craftsmanship required for that project.

That tradition has continued for over fifty years. Today, second- and third-generation artisans, descendants of the original artisans trained under Jorge Loyzaga, work for Loyzaga Studio. The masterful, esoteric skills of these craftspeople in fine woodwork, bronze casting, stone carving, decorative painting, and other trades are a source of great pride for them. It is a tacit knowledge, transferred hand-to-hand from master to apprentice in the ancient tradition. And though these skills and expertise are increasingly categorized as lost arts, they remain vital within the Loyzaga Studio.

In a shrinking, globalized world, where everything appears to resemble everything else and generic, prefabricated looks and styles prevail, it is refreshing to learn everything produced by Loyzaga Studio is crafted by hand under a master of the trade. The Loyzaga Studio workshops continue to thrive raising the level of knowledge and craft among Mexican artisans with positive economic impact for whole communities.

Attention to detail, fine craftsmanship, and curatorial integrity are also evident in Loyzaga Studio interior design projects. Because of his formidable knowledge of decorative arts, fabrics, upholstery, colors, and furnishings, Jorge Loyzaga has frequently advised the Mexican National Institute of Anthropology and History (INAH) on aesthetic and cultural aspects as well as lost methods of construction and restoration of historic properties. His restoration of the interior design for Chapultepec Castle for example, in conjunction with INAH, vividly illustrates the integrity of every Loyzaga Studio project. After extensive research and travel to Miramare, Maximilian's palace in Trieste, Italy, Loyzaga sourced original plans for the gardens of Chapultepec. He studied the botanical archeology and oversaw the restoration of the gardens.

In addition, after discovering various materials, fabrics, color chips, samples, and invoices stored in a heap, he realized Chapultepec Castle had been incorrectly decorated in the French taste. When the Habsburgs were at home there, it was decorated in the Austrian manner. Everything was changed to achieve historic accuracy true to the Habsburgs' fancy. The original textiles manufactured by Braquenié, Paris, now part of Pierre Frey, were remade for the restoration down to the gold threads in the curtains and sashes Carlota selected for window treatments loomed in the House of Lesach in Lyon, France.

Today, Jorge Loyzaga's legacy continues with the same integrity and curatorial excellence realized through Loyzaga Studio projects with his daughters, Sophia and Fernanda. Most likely, the final assessment of the Loyzaga Studio portfolio of houses will best be considered in aggregate where the full scope of Jorge Loyzaga's cohesive aesthetic vision is evident.

Without doubt, our domestic environments have profound impact upon our emotions and identity as Bachelard contended, as well as the way we live and who we are. A final consideration: Walter Gropius, founder of the Bauhaus school, introduced the idea of houses as machines for living, which may prove a prescient warning for the dehumanizing effect of efficiency and functionality that dogs contemporary life. In contrast, Jorge Loyzaga's humanistic approach through classical proportion and harmonics is linked with nature, geometry, and music. And as he maintains, the houses he designs are instruments for a gracious lifestyle that celebrates the art of living, which some consider the greatest art of all.

—Philip Alvaré

CASA
SAN ÁNGEL

The San Ángel house is located within a residential area
in the south section of Mexico City and an elegant
homage to classic Mexican architecture of the colonial
period, in the style of the eighteenth century.
Cobblestone streets in the district evoke the viceregal
era when Mexico was a jewel in the crown of the
Spanish Empire. The property faces to the street, and
great care was taken with landscape design to ensure
privacy and a sense of refuge within the urban context.

MEXICAN COLONIAL: CASA SAN ÁNGEL

A short run of stairs rises to the front façade with a carved limestone portico ensconced in greenery. The solid-wood front door under a beamed-tiled roof evokes the style of the period. Within, a handsome pair of wrought iron gates define the traditional *zaguán*, or entrance vestibule, delimiting public and private areas.

Arabesque geometries carved on the vestibule doors hint at the interior where an elaborately coffered ceiling in the sixteenth-century Mudéjar style—a fusion of Ibero, Gothic, and Islamic architecture used extensively throughout Mexico during the colonial period—spans the living and dining area.

It was of utmost importance to the clients that their residence project a Mexican aesthetic and all materials were sourced nationally. The overall plan is true to the period and style with rooms arranged around a U-shaped, glass-enclosed, colonnaded courtyard—the epicenter of family activity. Contemporary adaptations include a soda fountain, games room, and two-story library where the owners and their sons entertain friends.

Jorge Loyzaga collaborated closely with the clients to realize all elements of design and decoration, forging a lasting friendship with the renowned doctor and his wife, a well-known psychologist and philosopher. Much of the furnishings and decorations were made by Loyzaga Studio artisans. The masterfully crafted, finely carved wood paneling throughout achieves a summit of refinement in the library.

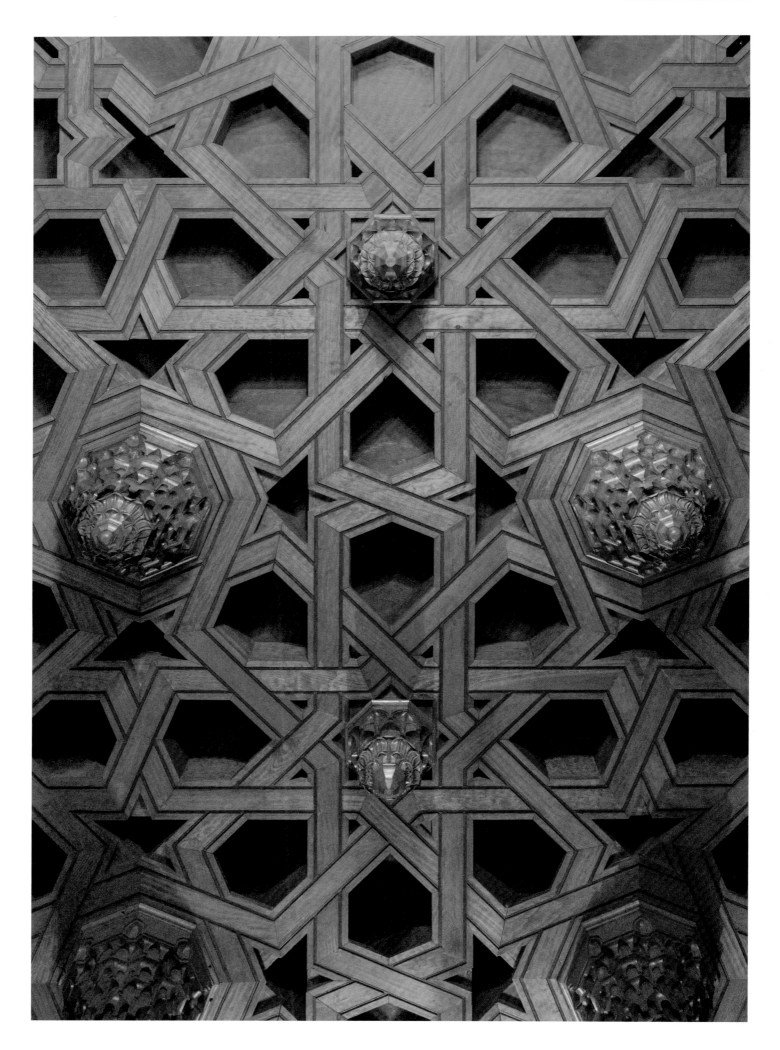

I had an agreement with the clients that from wherever they stopped and turned in the house they would perceive an aesthetic imprint, there had to be beauty.

–J.L.

Casa San Ángel's central patio can be considered the soul of the house. The furniture and chandeliers were custom designed by Loyzaga for this project, as well as the cedar wood Mudéjar ceiling (page 20).

FRENCH MANOIR: ÎLE-DE-FRANCE

The panoply of slate-clad mansard roofs beckons the visitor. Elegantly landscaped gardens embrace the property. A dining area on the terrace alongside the loggia has commanding views of the Sierra Madre Mountains evoking images of evenings under the stars, fetes of which Proust might have approved.

The handsome limestone façade of the main entrance is anchored by paving stones patterned as a square within a circle, a classical geometric form—a Loyzaga Studio signature. The fine wrought iron grille set within a Romanesque arch at the front door is flanked by a pair of antique sconces surmounted by a second-story window framed by double-columned pilasters. Copper downspouts add delightfully functional ornamentation.

Inlaid marble floors and masterfully crafted woodwork throughout the house recall period style, though the layout was adapted from a traditional eighteenth-century plan to accommodate the owners, a young couple with three children. They wanted a home revolving around the husband's passion for cooking and the wife's finesse at hosting sparkling events.

The result, a two-story kitchen, a cold storage room, and fully stocked pantry equipped with an impressive array of tableware, silver cutlery, and fine linens. Kitchen appliances are from La Cornue. An impressively scaled antique Dutch, four-tier brass chandelier illuminates the culinary environment.

The stained glass ceiling in the dining room was sourced at auction in New York City. A twenty-six-foot-long bar confirms the celebratory spirit. The interior decoration was a collaborative effort between Jorge Loyzaga and the clients, with their extensive collection of furniture and decorative objects. The custom, black marble dining table is from Loyzaga Studio.

On opposite page, the dining room's Tiffany glass ceiling is an antique piece originally from The Russian Tea Room in New York City.

CASA
LA AVENTURA

Set within an extensive tract of land held for
generations within the same family, Casa La Aventura
is in Nuevo León, Mexico. The design is based upon
English Jacobean architecture combining period Gothic
and Renaissance elements. The distribution of social
areas and bedrooms is extended on the ground floor,
which includes a circular library, trophy room, and
colonnaded corridors leading to terraces, a pool,
and pavilion.

ENGLISH JACOBEAN: CASA LA AVENTURA

A home theater spans the second story and a separate garage houses
a vintage automobile collection. The challenging weather extremes of
Northern Mexico were met with state-of-the-art, smart climate control
systems throughout the residence.

An inviting drive winds through an ancient-growth forest, lovingly preserved
by the owners, where remnants of a former hacienda once stood with a lake
and original gardens that were assiduously restored. A triple-arched portico of
sculpted limestone surmounted by a tympanum of half-timbered wood greets
the visitor at the entrance. A chapel with a Gothic arch, belfry, and eighteenth-
century Mexican colonial cross flanks the main residence. The clients grew
enamored of Jacobean architecture during their time spent in England.

Regional *vallecillo* stone used for the exterior is evident within the portico
where a hand-carved front door based upon a period Jacobean design opens
into a front foyer with a sense of ecclesiastic serenity. The vaulted-arch
ceiling of meticulously carved limestone supported by double columns rises
from highly polished inlaid marble floors. Murals and trompe l'oeil details
embellish design elements. A coffered dome ceiling with an oculus in the
double-height library recalls the Pantheon in Rome. The Gothic, hammer-
beam ceiling in the living room is a triumph of the art of joinery and fine
woodcarving. All architecture, interior design, and decorative elements
were masterfully realized by Jorge Loyzaga and Loyzaga Studio artisans and
harmoniously integrated with pieces from the client's ancestral collection.

The Gothic hammer-beam ceiling in the living room is a triumph of the art of joinery and fine woodcarving.

Jacobean style is a mixture of Gothic and Renaissance period styles, and the echo and harmonious marriage of these two styles can be seen throughout this house.

—J.L.

On previous pages, the coffered dome ceiling with an oculus in the two-story library recalls the Pantheon in Rome.

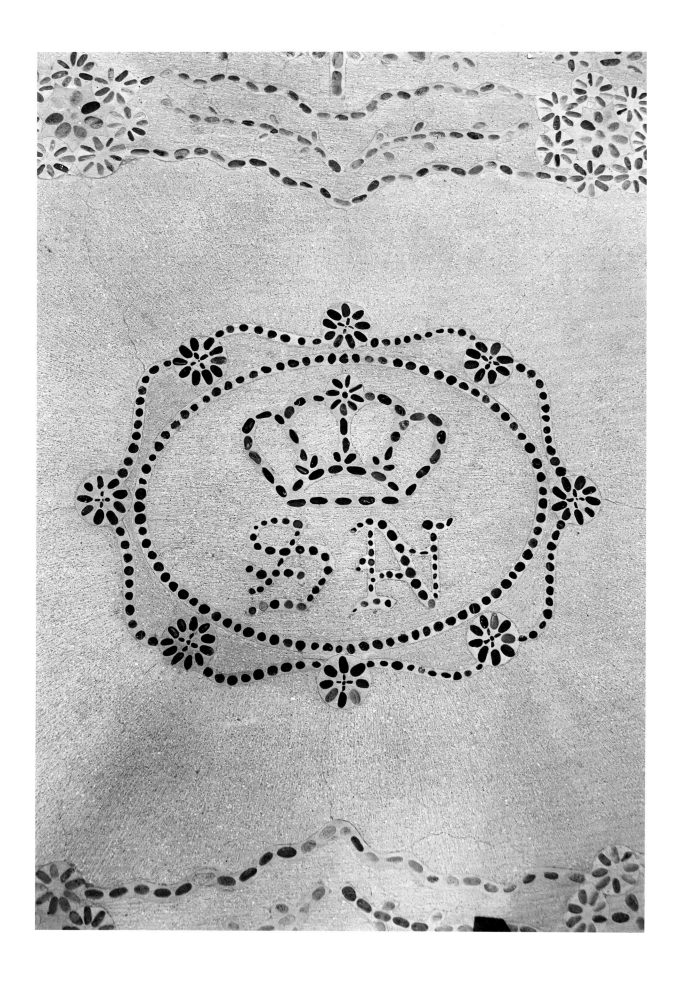

This house is the reflection of the romance from my travels in Asia; it represents the great Western country that New Spain created in Southeast Asia.

—J.L.

On previous pages, the original Philippine wooden structure from the eighteenth century occupies the second floor of the house. The sliding windows are made in the traditional style of the time, with capiz shells instead of glass.

Some eighteenth- and nineteenth-century Philippine furnishings and objets d'art from the notable collection of the owners.

Most of the furnishings and accessories in this residence are antiques from the Philippines.

*The inlaid marble floors of the Italian
palaces, whether composed of square- or
diamond-shaped blocks, or decorated
with a large design in different colors,
are unsurpassed in beauty.*

—*Edith Wharton,*
The Decoration of Houses

On previous pages, a series of galleries surround the main courtyard
with custom-made carpets from Aubusson and hand-painted Pompeian
frescoes designed by Loyzaga, in the Italian eighteenth-century manner.
On opposite page, a circular lily pool evokes the elegance of the
Enlightenment. A bronze copy of the sculpture *Mercurio Volante* by
Giambologna crowns it.

The ornate trompe l'oeil treillage on the arched ceiling of one of the many loggias is worthy of attention. On following pages, a Flemish tapestry from the eighteenth century, in the grand salon.

CASA
LA CEIBA

The Casa La Ceiba is well positioned within an
English garden in a leafy, long-established residential
neighborhood of Mexico City notable for its ancient-
growth trees. The overall design was based upon the
early twentieth-century, French beaux arts style with
art deco influences evident in decorative elements and
details throughout the handsome residence.

FRENCH BEAUX ARTS: CASA LA CEIBA

The plan was developed around a central, two-story domed hall from which the principal social areas are distributed. A direct entrance from the street leads to the front façade with a portico clad in carved white, Pachuca limestone from Mexico. Wrought iron balustrades, railings, and the sconces flanking the front door, as well as the ornate frieze and decorative devices, convey iconic, art deco style. Many of the decorative elements, such as lighting fixtures, door handles, and fine woodwork, were designed by Jorge Loyzaga and manufactured by Loyzaga Studio artisans in Mexico City. Additional period art deco furniture, lamps, and decorative objects were sourced in New York City.

A well-known entrepreneur, the owner is a patron of the arts and lifelong colleague and friend of Jorge Loyzaga. Their shared love for the preservation and support of the arts and culture forged a keen alliance. They have successfully collaborated on numerous projects over the years as evidenced by the successful synthesis of contemporary and period works of art and decorations that blend harmoniously within this classically proportioned residence.

A particular fascination with the art and architecture of India is reflected in the elaborate Mughal-style architrave in the spacious games room and dining area where the owner takes breakfast and receives close friends. The heroically scaled bronze lotus basin fountain strikes a transitional note toward the open terrace with an awning overlooking the garden. The neoclassical pavilion with a glass-domed ceiling within the garden suggests a temple of Venus and is nestled among perennial drifts alongside a pond.

An antique French keystone was adapted to the portal design. On opposite page, *Trompettiste* sculptures by Ferdinand Parpan. On following pages, antique Indian columns and basin were integrated to the room's design.

This house is a happy marriage between French architecture of the early twentieth century, circa 1910, and the subsequent art deco style that began in the 1920s.

—J.L.

On previous pages, important Latin American artists comprise the house's art collection: in the background, in the salon, the painting *Menina after Velazquez* by Fernando Botero and in the living room, the screen *Biombo Serpenteado* by Rodolfo Morales.
On following pages, an art deco inspired door made out of wood marquetry and bronze, designed by Loyzaga.

LA GIRALDA

Built on a ravine, La Giralda is located within a
residential enclave of Mexico City. The design is based
upon English neoclassical architecture of the eighteenth
century with an eclectic mix of contemporaneous
French and Mexican design elements.

MEXICAN COLONIAL: LA GIRALDA

Because of its dramatic site, the entrance to the classically proportioned property is on the top floor, and social areas, including a living room, dining room, and library, are on the ground floor overlooking the gardens.

A steeply inclined cobblestone drive leads to a small square in front of a triple-arched, carved limestone façade and entablature with a handsome wrought iron grille at the entrance. The unique arrangement of a second façade, with a boldly arched eighteenth-century Mexican door surround, within what is now a spacious entrance hall, was originally the front façade. The expansive space was the result of a later addition on the steeply sloped site to create a playroom and entertainment center for the client's children.

The entrepreneur and his wife, a gallery owner from New York City, share a passion for antiques as evidenced by their extensive collection of European and Mexican furniture, paintings, and objet d'art from the eighteenth and nineteenth centuries. Their collaboration with Jorge Loyzaga in the design and decoration of La Giralda was harmonious due to their shared enthusiasm for the neoclassical style of the eighteenth century across various cultures as well as the architect's profound knowledge of the period.

As a result, a shell-shaped niche above a window in the library, a traditional Mexican decorative element, achieves harmony with finely realized wood paneling in the English taste. A French beaux arts fireplace surround with fluted columns blends elegantly with eighteenth-century Mexican Poblana neoclassical marquetry furniture—prized for its superb quality and the richness of the inlaid wood. And fine nineteenth-century Mexican paintings combine seamlessly with contemporary works of art.

On previous pages, an original stone *portada* and door from
a monastery in Zacatecas.

La Giralda is the result of a combination of the clients' passion as art and antiques collectors—a process that never ends and always surprises with new acquisitions, and an architecture that brings cohesiveness to all the various elements.

—J.L.

An extensive collection of European and Mexican furniture, paintings, and objets d'art from the eighteenth and nineteenth centuries is combined with contemporary works of art. For example, a French beaux arts fireplace, originally from a *casona* in Colonia Roma, sits in the library below the painting *Dos Personajes en Uno* by Rufino Tamayo (page 114).
In the living room, the painting *Retrato de Lupe Marín* by Juan Soriano, between the two windows, provides a focal point; on the left, a painting by Luis García Guerrero (pages 110–111).

115

SANSSOUCI

Sanssouci is ensconced deep within the mountain forest of Cumbres de Monterrey National Park in the north of Mexico. The design is based upon French Napoleon III style architecture from the second half of the nineteenth century. The splendid, two-story residence was created around a central dome with a cupola flanked by symmetrical wings.

FRENCH NAPOLEON III: SANSSOUCI

Sans souci means without worry—a fitting name for the weekend retreat
of a renowned entrepreneur and matriarch of a prominent family who sought
a refuge where she could graciously entertain guests and family members.

The striking villa with commanding fenestration emerges as a sanctuary
within the woodland setting. The elegant façade of masterfully carved limestone
was quarried in San Luis Potosí, Mexico. Intricate carving and ornamental
devices on the cornices, frieze, and pilasters are testament to the expertise of
Loyzaga Studio artisans. The bold geometric flourish at the entrance plaza
comprised of patterned blocks confirms the Loyzaga signature. The stained
glass, domed ceiling, and dramatic black-and-white marble floor in
the main foyer make a memorable graphic impression.

Jorge Loyzaga designed the client's principal residence in the 1980s and
Sanssouci was a subsequent commission. Great care was taken to ensure
the owner's formidable collection of art, antiques, and decorative elements
were harmoniously integrated within the architectural environment. The
extraordinary, clear "cathedral glass" dome in the grand salon was created
by artisans from Torreón, Mexico, renowned for their craft, while the armature
to support the glass was manufactured by Loyzaga Studio artisans in
Monterrey, Mexico.

A dazzling array of chandeliers illuminates numerous social areas throughout
the house where frequent, sparkling family functions and graciously hosted
events take place. The chandeliers at the entrance of the living room are from
the Cristalleries Saint-Louis; another in the study is Baccarat. The French
stained glass window in the Napoleon III style for the entrance hall was
commissioned in Paris.

The vast collection of fine and decorative arts, some inherited and others sourced specifically for the creation of Sanssouci, confers the qualifications for a museum.

—J.L.

Great care was taken to ensure that the owner's formidable collection of art, antiques, and decorative elements were harmoniously integrated within the architectural environment. In the entrance hall, the nineteenth-century style vitraux was custom made in France for the space (page 119). On opposite page, the extraordinary, clear "cathedral glass" dome in the grand salon was designed by Loyzaga and created by artisans from Torreón, Mexico (also pages 128–129). On the wall, *Luna Lunatica*, a series of five paintings commissioned to the Mexican artist Alejandro Colunga specially for this room.

CASA GARUDA

Casa Garuda was constructed on a vast platform
high in the foothills of the Sierra Madre Mountains
in northern Mexico. Based upon the extensive studies
of renowned British architect, Sir Edwin Lutyens,
the design is true to Indian Mughal architecture of the
eighteenth century realized through Jorge Loyzaga's
exacting knowledge of the period.

INDIAN MUGHAL: **CASA GARUDA**

An apropos appellation for the Mughal fantasy, a Garuda is a mythological creature, half human, half eagle, that symbolizes birth and heaven.

The approach down a long, tree-lined drive affords glimpses of the imaginative residence that revolves around an octagonal, cupola-crowned rotunda and center of the house, with eight surrounding naves radiating into different social areas. Water spilling from the petals of a tiered Mughal fountain at the entrance strikes a tranquil note. One nave of the house opens onto a spacious loggia overlooking a pool and gardens fit for a Raj. Though constructed over thirty years ago, the serenely harmonic design is timeless.

A consummate collector of Indian art and decorative objects, the owner has traveled extensively throughout India since childhood. Her love of the culture is reflected in myriad ways throughout the residence. Ornate window lattices and brass lanterns crafted by Loyzaga Studio artisans are artfully combined with extraordinary pieces imported from India, including ornate chandeliers, fine antique furniture, decorative doors fit for a palace, and sumptuous fabrics that enhance the ethereal domain.

Jorge Loyzaga worked diligently with the client who readily admits she feels most at home in India, wears lavish silk saris, and is often encountered serving Darjeeling tea from an Indian tea set on a lacquered wood tray encrusted with mother-of-pearl. The result of their collaboration yielded an aesthetic harmony and cohesive balance between the client's extensive collections and the architectural environment, which achieves a near-otherworldly presence and complete surrender to India, echoed in every element.

Entering Casa Garuda is like entering a Mughal fantasy, which is gracefully visible in every detail and reflects the owner's personality as well.

—*J.L.*

The octagonal, cupola-crowned rotunda and center of the house is surrounded by eight naves radiating into different social areas (pages 135 and 136–137).

Original Indian doors made out of wood and shells were integrated in Loyzaga's design for the dining room, as well as a crystal Indian chandelier and centerpiece (pages 142–143).

VILLA TOSCANA

Villa Toscana is located in the foothills of the Eastern
Sierra Madre Mountains in northern Mexico on a large
tract of land encompassing an extended family compound.
The design is based upon classically proportioned
Italian Tuscan villas from the sixteenth century.

The grand estate revolves around a main courtyard
where a lily pool, parterre gardens, and breathtaking
mountain views complete the Renaissance idyll.

ITALIAN TUSCAN: VILLA TOSCANA

An inclined drive leads to a circular plaza with geometrically patterned paving blocks inspired by Sebastiano Serlio, the Italian mannerist architect who championed classical proportions. The columned, limestone portico with a semicircular pediment at the entrance embodies the spirit of the Cinquecento. A stylistically similar structure across the plaza cleverly conceals a cistern and source of water for the entire property.

The coffered ceiling in the front foyer offers striking accompaniment to an inlaid, colored marble floor and pair of trompe l'oeil faux marble niches. Principal social areas arranged on the ground floor include a glassed-in gallery leading to the gardens. The second floor occupies a smaller footprint allowing space for a two-story library annexed to the main bedroom. The library offers sanctuary apart from lively family gatherings for the client who has a PhD in Education. The pool and spacious neoclassical-inspired pool house were designed to accommodate frequent family fiestas.

When Jorge Loyzaga created Villa Toscana over thirty years ago, it was one of his largest commissions and a triumph of classical harmony and proportion. From mural paintings and mosaics to architectural and decorative detail throughout, the elegant residence is true to Tuscan style. A coffered ceiling with octagonal *casetones* and lively tapestry wall coverings from Rubelli in the living room evoke the flair of sixteenth-century Italian style. The successful collaboration between Jorge Loyzaga and the clients blossomed into additional commissions with subsequent generations and members of the extended family.

Villa Toscana has served as the cradle for generations of fraternal and family traditions built around its main patio.

—J.L.

The coffered ceiling in the front foyer offers striking accompaniment to an inlaid, colored marble floor and pair of trompe l'oeil faux marble niches.

The carved stone vaulted ceiling in the entrance hall in the Gothic taste, and finely handcrafted medieval-style wood ceilings throughout, evoke the charm of the period. A carved limestone Tudor fireplace surround with shield devices in the games room rises to a height of nearly twenty feet.

LOS AZAHARES

Los Azahares boasts panoramic perspectives from its mountainside position overlooking the northern part of Monterrey. The handsome residence was designed around a central courtyard in the manner of urban architecture from the viceregal colonial period in Mexico during the eighteenth century. When in bloom, four orange trees arranged in a quadrant around a baroque fountain in the courtyard produce blossoms —*los azahares* in Spanish—that perfume the air.

MEXICAN COLONIAL: LOS AZAHARES

The drive leads to paving stones at the stately front façade with window surrounds and a portico of carved limestone quarried from San Luis Potosí, Mexico, with its characteristic russet hue. The masterfully carved cedar wood door at the entrance, true to the period, opens directly onto the central courtyard. Elegantly colonnaded galleries surround the monastic enclosure and give access to social areas with bedrooms and sitting rooms arranged on the second floor.

Jorge Loyzaga gave form to the client's fascination with eighteenth-century viceregal architecture of central Mexico in a variety of ways that reflect traditions of the era. The vaulted brick oven with grille burners and the Talavera tiles from Puebla decorating walls in the kitchen are time-honored period elements. Fine joinery and wood paneling deftly crafted by Loyzaga Studio artisans in the two-story library are in the English taste, while the ceiling is Hispano-Arabic Mudéjar. A separate trophy room was created for the husband, an avid huntsman. The lively painting of wedding festivities at a country estate in the dining room, after the original in Chapultepec Castle, celebrates a sybaritic viceregal scene.

Multiple terraces open onto intimate, themed gardens surrounding the house, integrating interior and exterior environments. The harmonious balance between nature and architecture is further enhanced with masterfully executed foliate mural paintings throughout the residence. A superbly painted trompe l'oeil trellised archway with exuberant vines, flowers, and birds overlooks one of the theme gardens and provides sanctuary on summer mornings.

189

It is extraordinary and fortunate to work with a team of craftsmen whose enthusiasm matches that of the clients' as well as the architect and allows us to collaborate and achieve this fine level of work.

—J.L.

In the central courtyard, the carved-stone Mexican fountain, typical of Mexican interior courtyards of the eighteenth century, was custom designed by Loyzaga and handcrafted by Mexican artisans (pages 184–185). In the dining room, a custom-made hand-painted screen represents a marriage scene in a Mexican formal garden of the eighteenth century (pages 186–187). The harmonious balance between nature and architecture is further enhanced with masterfully executed foliate mural paintings throughout the residence.

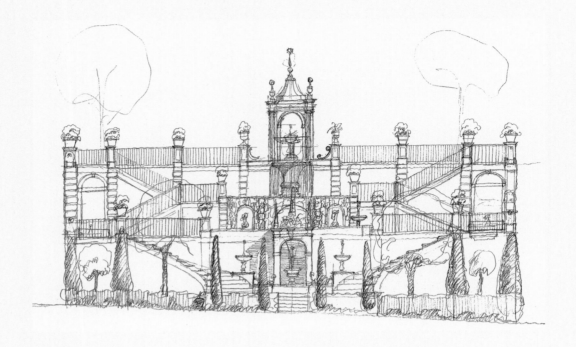

SANTUARIO

Santuario is a stately French beaux arts manor with
a commanding mountaintop position facing north
above the city of Monterrey, Mexico, with a panoramic
perspective. The design is based upon the classical
decorative style of the nineteenth-century École des
Beaux-Arts in Paris, and its more eclectic architectural
interpretation in England and the United States at
the turn of the nineteenth and twentieth centuries.
It is reminiscent of the grand summer "cottages"
constructed during the Gilded Age in Newport,
Rhode Island, circa 1900.

FRENCH BEAUX ARTS: SANTUARIO

Handsome gates on the street signal the entrance to the property with a
sloping drive to the front façade of carved white limestone from the Pachuca
region of Mexico. The longitudinal plan is principally on one floor with
separate guest accommodations on a second story. The rectilinear portico
with Tuscan columns, balustrade, and coigned edges echoes the Newport set's
penchant for classical order. The black slate roof tiles were sourced in Spain.

The prominent entrepreneur and political figure and his wife wanted
a home designed to accommodate children and grandchildren and host
multigenerational festivities. Jorge Loyzaga worked closely with them to
create spacious facilities for entertaining, including a large pool and barbecue
area, a cabin for events, and an expansive platform where weddings with
over 1,000 guests have taken place.

The interior design reflects the clients' traditional and gracious way of life
including a reception room apart from the living area to receive "callers"
in keeping with Anglo-American customs. A delightfully eclectic mix of
antique and contemporary furnishings—some inherited, others acquired or
crafted by Loyzaga Studio artisans—project the agreeable comfort of English
country houses. Terraced French parterre gardens evoke Le Notre's green
geometries at Versailles with belvederes placed strategically to take advantage
of the spectacular views, dramatic sunsets, and reflective moments on
moonlit evenings.

A delightfully eclectic mix of antique and contemporary furnishings
—some inherited, others acquired or crafted by Loyzaga Studio artisans.
The English-style marble fireplace and a handcrafted stucco ceiling are
the main focal points of the salon. A painting by Rodolfo Morales, above
the chimney and one by Benjamín Domínguez, on the right, punctuate
the room (pages 202–203).
On opposite page, the English-style informal dining room with boiseries
and colors used typically in the eighteenth century.
On following pages, the formal and terraced garden, inspired by European
classical gardens like the ones of Versailles and on the Amalfi Coast.

LOS ÁNGELES
DEL MAR

On a hillside soaring high above the bay in Acapulco, Mexico, Los Ángeles del Mar was inspired by nineteenth-century palaces and sanctuaries in Bali.

Twelve separate structures linked through a network of platforms and elegantly colonnaded corridors revolve around a central pavilion that houses principal social areas including a living room, dining room, kitchen, and main bedroom suite. Smaller pavilions distributed around a large pond, which serves as a unifying water element, contain individual guest suites with private pools and gardens.

BALINESE STYLE: LOS ÁNGELES DEL MAR

The design was developed to accommodate multiple generations of a large, extended family on weekends and holiday occasions.

The approach through a pair of highly carved wood gates leads to an archway at the entrance of the central pavilion reminiscent of a Balinese temple. The owners' passion for Bali is reflected in an expansive collection of works of art, antiques, and decorative elements acquired during extensive travel and now harmoniously integrated within the serenely proportioned architectural environment. Their lifelong affiliation with Jorge Loyzaga, combined with his profound knowledge of Southeast Asian art and architecture, proved a fruitful collaboration evident in every detail. Great care was taken to ensure authenticity in period and style.

Satin-like wall surfaces of whitewashed stucco made with sand and lime and superbly carved and crafted wood joinery as well as painstakingly realized structural elements—most notably in the ceiling details—were created in the traditional Southeast Asian manner by Loyzaga Studio artisans. Bali remained a Dutch colony for over 600 years, and the clay roof tiles, produced in Monterrey, Mexico, in a vernacular Netherlands style assert the integrity of craftsmanship and design. Additional architectural and decorative elements such as carved-stone mosaic floor designs and murals reflect a confluence of Asian and Arab influences as well as Jorge Loyzaga's astute understanding of Balinese aesthetics.

Detail of the exterior shower made out of local shells.

221

LOS ARCÁNGELES

Set within the eastern range of the Sierra Madre
Mountains in Monterrey, Mexico, Los Arcángeles
combines Mexican colonial and neoclassical
architectural styles. The site was selected within
the client's extensive ranch, and the rugged terrain
was leveled and landscaped with a lake.
The house was designed to ensure bedrooms
and social areas had water views.

MEXICAN NEOCLASSICAL: LOS ARCÁNGELES

A path lined with indigenous oak trees leads to the front entrance plaza where the family chapel greets the visitor. Formal gardens with clipped boxwood hedges and columnar cypress trees provide the perfect foil for a pavilion, social area, and rose varieties. An 8,000-square-foot gallery—a veritable museum of fine and decorative arts—houses the client's private collection.

Los Arcángeles was designed and constructed thirty-five years ago, and the process forged an enduring friendship between Jorge Loyzaga and the clients. Their shared passion for history, art, architecture—especially the Asiatic influence on Mexican art of the viceregal period—is evident throughout. The staggering collection includes Chinese export porcelain, ecclesiastical works of art (notably a collection of eighteenth-century Mexican paintings of archangels), and fine antique furniture from the eighteenth century.

The grand entrance hall with an inlaid marble floor and ornate, barrel-vault ceiling includes an oratory. An eighteenth-century Portuguese center table and superb garniture set of seventeenth-century Chinese porcelain urns are presented in front of a niche with a Japanese screen. Ornamental plasterwork in the living room and masterfully carved wood door surrounds throughout the house certify the Loyzaga signature.

The dining room seats twenty-four and boasts a ceiling encrusted with seventeenth-century, late-Ming, blue-and-white plates. A palatially scaled Russian crystal chandelier illuminates frequent extended family gatherings, which include baptisms and weddings in the chapel where a giltwood altarpiece and original hand-painted ceiling and walls were modeled after chapels in Sintra, Portugal.

Formal gardens with clipped boxwood hedges and columnar cypress trees
provide the perfect foil for a pavilion.

On previous pages, the grand entrance hall opens on an inlaid marble floor and ornate, barrel-vault ceiling. On the eighteenth-century Portuguese center table, the superb garniture set of seventeenth-century Chinese porcelain urns; in the back, the niche hosts a Japanese screen.

In the twenty-four-seat dining room, the ceiling is encrusted with
seventeenth-century late-Ming, blue-and-white plates; a Russian crystal
chandelier takes center stage of the room.

GLORIA IN EXCELSIS DEO

LVX ORTA EST

A giltwood altarpiece and original hand-painted ceiling and walls decorate
the chapel, modeled after chapels in Sintra, Portugal.

VILLA NAPOLITANA

Villa Napolitana appears suspended between sea and sky on a cliff's edge above the bay in Acapulco, Mexico. The design was inspired by Italian baroque Neapolitan villas of the seventeenth century when Naples was part of the Spanish Empire.

The classically proportioned residence revolves around a central courtyard with an impluvium—a square pool at the center based on ancient Roman rainwater catchments—adapted as a fountain with dancing-water jets. Elegant, sculpture-filled colonnaded corridors around the courtyard give way to social areas on the ground floor.

ITALIAN BAROQUE: VILLA NAPOLITANA

A plunging drive down from the road leads to a plaza at the villa's entrance where an ivory-colored portico of hand-carved sandstone quarried in Puebla is flanked by a pair of antique marble lions. The rust red, burnt sienna color of the façade and interior walls, true to period and style, was achieved with *cal*— powdered lime mixed with natural sienna earth pigment, rich in iron oxide. An intricately scrolled, Italianate wrought iron front door set in a Romanesque arch affords glimpses into the airy expanse within, where a semicircular staircase creates stately communication between the ground floor and second-story bedrooms. Entirely open social areas and bedrooms are plein air with superb cross-ventilation and spectacular ocean views.

A third-generation Loyzaga Studio client, the owner had been enamored of Acapulco since childhood with fond memories of his grandfather's Italian neoclassical villa there—also designed by Jorge Loyzaga. The prominent businessman envisioned a similar retreat in which to enjoy extended stays by the seashore. Superbly executed architectural and decorative details, masterfully crafted by Loyzaga Studio artisans, provide a harmonious context for inherited and acquired furnishings and decorations. Inlaid colored marble floors with spirited geometric patterns—a Loyzaga signature—evoke Neapolitan reveries. The image of the sea and sky reflected in the infinity pool running the entire length of the seafront property merge into an endless horizon.

This house, with its architecture, color, and magic has the power to transport you to any part of the southern Italian península.

—J.L.

On previous page, an intricately scrolled, Italianate wrought iron front door designed by Loyzaga and flanked by two Italian lions, affords glimpses into the airy expanse within where a semicircular staircase creates stately communication between the ground and second floors.

EL CARMEN
DE LA SIERRA

Located within Chipinque National Park
in the foothills of the Sierra Madre Mountains of
northern Mexico, the design for El Carmen de la Sierra
was inspired by traditional Mexican plantation houses
of the eighteenth century. The name, *El Carmen*,
suggests a retreat among the orchards and gardens
of a grand country estate.

MEXICAN COLONIAL: EL CARMEN DE LA SIERRA

Principal social areas and bedrooms are distributed within a central rectangular block, while a perimeter of colonnaded galleries surrounds the entire hacienda affording stunning mountain vistas and romantic views of low-lying valleys from every perspective.

The long, winding, tree-lined drive leads to a plaza where a stately arcade of carved sandstone arches and columns runs the entire length of the front façade. The traditional Mexican garden at the entrance, punctuated with contemporary sculpture, is one of many designed by Jorge Loyzaga on terraces throughout the property. One includes a small lake with koi; another, a pool and pavilions for entertaining. The front door is hand carved of historically accurate red cedar wood. It was of utmost importance to the clients that their home reflects an aesthetic integrity true to eighteenth-century Mexican architecture and decoration.

Extensive research of period customs and interior design informed the distribution of rooms and arrangement of contemporaneous furniture and objets d'art from the clients' family collection. Many additional design elements such as decorative mural paintings and the extraordinary Mudéjar ceiling in the living room, which took a year to create, were crafted by Loyzaga Studio artisans. The vaulted ceiling of the spacious dining room is made of handmade moldings embellished with traditional Talavera pottery. Though the seigneurial residence was commissioned over thirty years ago, Jorge Loyzaga has maintained a close affiliation with the family and continued projects over generations include a chapel currently under construction with adequate acoustics for concerts, operas, and family festivities.

Sculptures by Leonora Carrington, *The Palmist*, and by Daniel Serna, in the garden (pages 254–255). On opposite page, *Hombre Ante El Paisaje* and *Boda Tarasca* by Pablo O'Higgins surround a painting by Rodolfo Morales.

LAS ÁGUILAS

From its magisterial position within a forest at
the foothills of the mountains in Monterrey, Mexico,
Las Águilas was designed in the English Tudor style of
the fourteenth century. The plan was developed along
a straight line with different sections in the English
medieval manner. The client's appreciation for
Tudor architecture was kindled during his university
days, and he envisioned a residence echoing the style
and sensibility of the period.

ENGLISH TUDOR: LAS ÁGUILAS

A tree-lined drive through a large tract of land leads to the main residence and hunting pavilion arranged around a square reminiscent of a carriage yard. Principally constructed of cut fieldstone, contrasting window surrounds and porticos at the main entrance and the hunting pavilion are masterfully carved of limestone in the Gothic taste. A delightful assortment of patterned-brick chimney pots crown English terracotta tiles on the gabled rooflines. An eagle finial, an *águila*—the eponymous symbol—crests a cupola.

Preliminary construction of the two-story manor occurred in the 1990s. Subsequent projects included a pool with pavilion, games room, and octagonal library with superb wood paneling in the Georgian style. Gardens were designed following Tudor sensibility with a lake, rose garden, potager, and chapel in the tradition of venerable English country houses. The owner, a prominent entrepreneur and avid huntsman, received the coveted Weatherby Award for his work in the field of hunting and conservation. His wife, a celebrated hostess and patron of the arts, renowned for elegant entertainment with heads of state and leading cultural figures, engaged Lady Henrietta Spencer-Churchill for the development of the interior design and decoration.

The stained glass bay window with a medieval theme set within a carved-stone, Gothic frame with pierced quatrefoils is especially notable. As well, Jorge Loyzaga's rigorous attention to architectural and decorative details based upon historical documentation of period style is realized throughout the residence in harmonious proportion with exquisite materials sourced entirely in Mexico, all expertly crafted by Loyzaga Studio artisans.

*The historical originality and integrity
of this house is such that all of the interior
and exterior architectural details were
documented for posterity.*

—J.L.

Jorge Loyzaga's rigorous attention to architectural and decorative details
based upon historical documentation of period style is realized throughout
the residence in harmonious proportion with exquisite materials sourced
entirely in Mexico. In the octagonal wood-paneled library, an English-style
marble fireplace, handcrafted in Mexico (pages 278–279).

Acknowledgments

I am deeply grateful and proud of all the effort and enthusiasm my dear daughter Sophia Loyzaga Palm put into this book; she is the driving force and soul of this project.

My heartfelt thanks to my wife Charlotte Choumenkovitch who is my soulmate and ideal companion—I would not be the person I am without her unconditional support.

I am very thankful to my daughter Fernanda Loyzaga Palm, who with her sister Sophia, will keep my work and studio's legacy alive.

A special thanks and appreciation to Mauricio de la Garza Clariond who is an excellent photographer and human being. Through his lens he captured the essence of classical architecture and the hidden symphony that it radiates.

My appreciation to the late Mrs. Maria Cusi de Escandon, my studio's first client, for believing in me.

My most sincere thanks and recognition to all my clients who put their faith and trust in me to design their projects, as well as those who opened their homes in order to make this book possible.

I thank my architectural and decoration team in my studio: Juan Zavala Terrazas, Jose Adrian Conde, Maria Guadalupe Magos Cruz, Olivia Martinez Zárate, Ruben Antonio Zambrano Carranza, Javier Adrian Gasca Mendez, Cesar Alejandro Lopez Lopez, Adrian Fernando Sanchez Ramirez, Jose Raul Hurvina Aguilar, Sonia Helian Guerrero Muñoz, Christian Adair Estrada, and Reyna Rivas Aguirre, whose professionalism and talent contributed to build these projects.

A huge and heartfelt thanks to my dear and excellent artists and craftsmen who brought my ideas to life through their amazing skills and who shaped and formed my designs.

I also am grateful to my administrative team: Marcela Concepcion Viloria Arroyo, Myriam Carreon Antunez, and Guadalupe Araceli Hernandez Ildefonso, as well as to all the coordinators and administrators of the projects that were achieved thanks to their dedication and hard work.

Last but not least many thanks to Rizzoli and to Catherine Bonifassi, Vanessa Blondel, Sara Villa, and Philip Alvaré who made this dream become a book.

—Jorge Loyzaga

With special thanks to the Loyzaga Family (Jorge, Charlotte, Fernanda, and Sophia) for believing in my work, and to Loyzaga's clients for opening their doors to their private homes, and to my family for always supporting me.

And thanks to Catherine Bonifassi and Vanessa Blondel, and to the Rizzoli team for trusting my vision.

—Mauricio de la Garza Clariond

Jorge Loyzaga: Classical and Harmonic Proportions

First published in the United States of America in 2023 by
Rizzoli International Publications, Inc.
300 Park Avenue South, NY 10010
www.rizzoliusa.com

© 2023 Loyzaga Design

Photography © Mauricio de la Garza Clariond
Text © Philip Alvaré

Publisher: Charles Miers
Editorial Director: Catherine Bonifassi
Editor: Victorine Lamothe
Production Director: Maria Pia Gramaglia
Managing Editor: Lynn Scrabis
Proofreader: Sarah Stump

Art Direction: S A V V Y
Bernardo Dominguez and Lydia Rodríguez

Editorial Coordination: CASSI EDITION
Vanessa Blondel

ISBN: 978-0-8478-7367-8
Library of Congress Control Number: 2023934511
2023 2024 2025 2026 / 10 9 8 7 6 5 4 3 2 1
Printed in Italy

Visit us online:
Facebook.com/RizzoliNewYork
Twitter: @Rizzoli_Books
Instagram.com/RizzoliBooks
Pinterest.com/RizzoliBooks
Youtube.com/user/RizzoliNY
Issuu.com/Rizzoli